S

by Iain Gray

LangSyne
PUBLISHING
WRITING *to* REMEMBER

Lang**Syne**

PUBLISHING

WRITING *to* REMEMBER

79 Main Street, Newtongrange,
Midlothian EH22 4NA
Tel: 0131 344 0414 Fax: 0845 075 6085
E-mail: info@lang-syne.co.uk
www.langsyneshop.co.uk

Design by Dorothy Meikle
Printed by Printwell Ltd
© Lang Syne Publishers Ltd 2018

All rights reserved. No part of this publication may be reproduced, stored or introduced into a retrieval system, or transmitted in any form or by any means (electronic, mechanical, photocopying, recording or otherwise) without the prior written permission of Lang Syne Publishers Ltd.

ISBN 978-1-85217-599-3

Smith

MOTTO:
By Divine Providence.

CREST:
A heron holding a fish in its beak.

NAME variations include:
Smyth
Smythe

Chapter one:

The origins of popular surnames

by George Forbes and Iain Gray

***If you don't know where you came from, you won't know where you're going** is a frequently quoted observation and one that has a particular resonance today when there has been a marked upsurge in interest in genealogy, with increasing numbers of people curious to trace their family roots.*

Main sources for genealogical research include census returns and official records of births, marriages and deaths – and the key to unlocking the detail they contain is obviously a family surname, one that has been 'inherited' and passed from generation to generation.

No matter our station in life, we all have surname – but it was not until about the middle of the fourteenth century that the practice of being identified by a particular surname became commonly established throughout the British Isles.

Previous to this, it was normal for a person to be identified through the use of only a forename.

But as population gradually increased and there were many more people with the same forename, surnames were adopted to distinguish one person, or community, from another.

Many common English surnames are patronymic in origin, meaning they stem from the forename of one's father – with 'Johnson,' for example, indicating 'son of John.'

It was the Normans, in the wake of their eleventh century conquest of Anglo-Saxon England, a pivotal moment in the nation's history, who first brought surnames into usage – although it was a gradual process.

For the Normans, these were names initially based on the title of their estates, local villages and chateaux in France to distinguish and identify these landholdings.

Such grand descriptions also helped enhance the prestige of these warlords and generally glorify their lofty positions high above the humble serfs slaving away below in the pecking order who had only single names, often with Biblical connotations as a Pierre and Jacques.

The only descriptive distinctions among the peasantry concerned their occupations, like 'Pierre the swineherd' or 'Jacques the ferryman.'

Roots of surnames that came into usage in England not only included Norman-French, but also Old French, Old Norse, Old English, Middle English, German, Latin, Greek, Hebrew and the Gaelic languages of the Celts.

The Normans themselves were originally Vikings, or 'Northmen', who raided, colonised and eventually settled down around the French coastline.

The had sailed up the Seine in their longboats in 900AD under their ferocious leader Rollo and ruled the roost in north eastern France before sailing over to conquer England in 1066 under Duke William of Normandy – better known to posterity as William the Conqueror, or King William I of England.

Granted lands in the newly-conquered England, some of their descendants later acquired territories in Wales, Scotland and Ireland – taking not only their own surnames, but also the practice of adopting a surname, with them.

But it was in England where Norman rule and custom first impacted, particularly in relation to the adoption of surnames.

This is reflected in the famous *Domesday Book*, a massive survey of much of England and Wales, ordered by William I, to determine who owned what, what it was worth and therefore how much they were liable to pay in taxes to the voracious Royal Exchequer.

Completed in 1086 and now held in the National Archives in Kew, London, 'Domesday' was an Old English word meaning 'Day of Judgement.'

This was because, in the words of one contemporary chronicler, "its decisions, like those of the Last Judgement, are unalterable."

It had been a requirement of all those English landholders – from the richest to the poorest – that they identify themselves for the purposes of the survey and for future reference by means of a surname.

This is why the *Domesday Book*, although written in Latin as was the practice for several centuries with both civic and ecclesiastical records, is an invaluable source for the early appearance of a wide range of English surnames.

Several of these names were coined in connection with occupations.

These include Baker and Smith, while Cooks, Chamberlains, Constables and Porters were to be found carrying out duties in large medieval households.

The church's influence can be found in names such as Bishop, Friar and Monk while the popular name of Bennett derives from the late fifth to mid-sixth century Saint Benedict, founder of the Benedictine order of monks.

The early medical profession is represented by Barber, while businessmen produced names that include Merchant and Sellers.

Down at the village watermill, the names that cropped up included Millar/Miller, Walker and Fuller, while other self-explanatory trades included Cooper, Tailor, Mason and Wright.

Even the scenery was utilised as in Moor, Hill, Wood and Forrest – while the hunt and the chase supplied names that include Hunter, Falconer, Fowler and Fox.

Colours are also a source of popular surnames as in Black, Brown, Gray/Grey, Green and White, and would have denoted the colour of the clothing the person habitually wore or, apart from the obvious exception of 'Green', one's hair colouring or even complexion.

The surname Red developed into Reid, while

Blue was rare and no-one wanted to be associated with yellow.

Rather self-important individuals took surnames that include Goodman and Wiseman, while physical attributes crept into surnames such as Small and Little.

Many families proudly boast the heraldic device known as a Coat of Arms, as featured on our front cover.

The central motif of the Coat of Arms would originally have been what was borne on the shield of a warrior to distinguish himself from others on the battlefield.

Not featured on the Coat of Arms, but highlighted on page three, is the family motto and related crest – with the latter frequently different from the central motif.

Adding further variety to the rich cultural heritage that is represented by surnames is the appearance in recent times in lists of the 100 most common names found in England of ones that include Khan, Patel and Singh – names that have proud roots in the vast sub-continent of India.

Echoes of a far distant past can still be found in our surnames and they can be borne with pride in commemoration of our forebears.

Chapter two:

Intrigue and conspiracy

Ranked at No. 1 in lists of the 100 most common surnames in England today, 'Smith' is of truly ancient origin.

An occupational name, it derives from the Old English 'smid', in turn derived from 'smitan' or 'smite', meaning to 'strike', in particular to strike with a hammer.

It came to be descriptive of not only those who worked as blacksmiths but also those employed in the crafting of precious metals into jewellery and other adornments.

A highly valued skill, those who would come to bear the Smith name have roots that stretch back to Anglo-Saxon times.

This means that flowing through the veins of many bearers of the name today may well be the blood of those Germanic tribes who invaded and settled in the south and east of the island of Britain from about the early fifth century.

Known as the Anglo-Saxons, they were composed of the Jutes, from the area of the Jutland

Peninsula in modern Denmark, the Saxons from Lower Saxony, in modern Germany and the Angles from the Angeln area of Germany.

It was the Angles who gave the name 'Engla land', or 'Aengla land' – better known as 'England.'

They held sway in what became England from approximately 550 until the Norman Conquest of 1066, with the main kingdoms those of Sussex, Wessex, Northumbria, Mercia, Kent, East Anglia and Essex.

Meanwhile, although by its very nature the occupation of working in metals was not confined to any one part of the British Isles, it is in modern-day County Durham, in North East England, that the name is particularly identified.

Those of the name who figure prominently in the often turbulent historical record, however, are recorded in many other locations.

Embroiled in late seventeenth century political intrigue and conspiracy, Aaron Smith was the English lawyer who only narrowly escaped execution for his role in an abortive attempt to assassinate Charles II and the Duke of York, the future James II.

Smith's place and date of birth are not known, but it is known that he was a member of the

Green Ribbon Club, founded in 1675 at the King's Head Tavern in Chancery Lane, London.

Composed of those politicians who would later become known as Whigs and other prominent figures, including Smith, its membership also included 'Dissenters' such as Presbyterians, Quakers, Baptists and Independents opposed to the form of Episcopacy that had been foisted on the Church of England.

Sporting green ribbons as a token of their membership of the club, their activities included not only the dissemination of Whig propaganda but also ceremonial public burnings, known as 'pope burnings', where an effigy of the pope would be consigned to a bonfire.

Smith was arrested in January of 1682 and hauled before the King's Bench on charges of disseminating seditious papers and making speeches disloyal to Charles II.

But he escaped custody and went into hiding before sentence could be pronounced.

He then became active behind the scenes in what became known as the Rye House Plot, a bungled attempt to ambush and kill Charles and the Duke of York in 1683 on their return from Newmarket to London.

The main conspirators, whose ultimate aim had been to place the king's illegitimate son, the Duke of Monmouth, on the throne, were quickly rounded up and executed.

Smith, meanwhile, who is thought to have acted as a liaison between groups of the ill-fated conspirators, was arrested and confined in the Tower of London.

But the wily lawyer had carefully covered his tracks and, to the frustration of the authorities, nothing could be conclusively proved against him.

He was, however, sentenced to the public humiliation of standing in the pillory for two hours and then to remain in prison 'pending security for good behaviour' for his previous offence of sedition.

He remained in prison until 1688 – the year of the 'Glorious Revolution' that saw James II, Charles II's successor, forced to flee into exile and his replacement on the throne by Duke William of Orange, as William III, and his wife Mary as Mary II.

Smith, ever the survivor, put forward claims for reward for his previous opposition to Charles II and James II and in April of 1689 William duly appointed him to the powerful and lucrative posts of solicitor to the treasury and later as public prosecutor.

It was this latter position that was to prove his undoing.

Tasked with prosecuting Jacobites, as sympathisers of the deposed James II were known, his conduct proved too much even for his own masters.

He was charged with fabricating the deposition of witnesses against alleged Jacobites and also falsifying his financial accounts to his own pecuniary advantage; dismissed in disgrace from all his posts, he died in 1701.

Another bearer of the Smith name who was also fortunate to escape execution was the London housebreaker John Smith, more popularly known as "Half-Hanged Smith", who managed to escape death by hanging on no fewer than three occasions.

Born in about 1661 in Malton, North Yorkshire, the son of a farmer, he served for a time in the Royal Navy and then the army, later embarking on his criminal career.

Sentenced to death in December of 1705 on two counts of housebreaking, he was hauled to the gallows at Tyburn, the noose put around his neck and hanged.

As he dangled in mid-air and slowly and painfully strangled to death, his family and friend attempted to alleviate his suffering by storming the gallows and frantically tugging on his legs to mercifully quicken the strangulation process.

But, after about quarter of an hour, Smith still clung tenaciously to life and the crowd cried out: "A reprieve!"

The reprieve was reluctantly, but duly, granted and Smith cut down and taken to a nearby house to recover.

Asked later how he had felt during his abortive 'execution', the bewildered Smith replied: "My spirits were in a great uproar, pushing upwards; when they got into my head I saw a great blaze of glaring light that seemed to go out of my head in a flash.

"Then the pain went. When I was cut down I got such pins-and-needles pains in my head that I could have hanged the people who set me free."

Officially granted a pardon in February of the following year, it was not long before he was again in the dock on housebreaking charges that would have led to his execution if found guilty.

But there were complex legal problems with the case and the jury had to leave the verdict to a panel of judges – who had no option but to set him free.

Undaunted by his narrow brushes with death, Smith some time later yet again faced execution after being found guilty of housebreaking.

But the prosecutor died before the day of the planned hanging and, again because of complex legal problems that arose from this, he was set free.

A number of years later, in May of 1727, Smith, under the alias of John Wilson, was found guilty of stealing a padlock and being found with eight padlock keys in his pocket.

It was charged that he and an accomplice had planned to break into and steal from a warehouse.

Found guilty of only the theft of the padlock he was sentenced to transportation to what was then the colony of Virginia – and subsequently disappeared from the historical record.

Chapter three:

Enterprise and politics

Celebrated today as the "Father of Modern Economics", Adam Smith was the Scottish pioneer of political economy and moral philosophy born in 1723 in Kirkcaldy, Fife.

The son of a senior advocate, solicitor and prosecutor, one colourful tale from his childhood is that when he was aged three he was abducted by gypsies and hurriedly released when a search party set off to find him.

After attending school in his native town he was aged only 14 when he entered Glasgow University – although this was not unusual at the time – to study moral philosophy, later taking postgraduate studies at Balliol College, Oxford.

It was while at Oxford that he took advantage of the magnificent collection of the Bodleian Library to educate himself on a diverse range of subjects.

This wealth of accumulated knowledge served him in great stead in later years when he penned his famous *An Inquiry into the Nature and Causes of the Wealth of Nations*, published in 1776 and more commonly known today as *The Wealth of Nations*.

The first modern work of economics and considered to have laid the foundations of free market economic theory, a copy is said to have been carried by former British Prime Minister Margaret Thatcher in her handbag.

A leading light during the intellectual ferment known as the Scottish Enlightenment and a friend and contemporary of other luminaries who included the philosopher David Hume, his other major work is the 1759 *The Theory of Moral Sentiments*.

Having held a number of top academic posts that included head of moral philosophy at his old alma mater of Glasgow University and one of the founding members of the Royal Society of Edinburgh, he died in 1790. Ironically, considering his great achievements, he is reputed to have lamented on his deathbed that he 'had not achieved enough.'

In keeping with the economic theory expounded by Adam Smith, one leading nineteenth century English entrepreneur was William Henry Smith.

Born in 1792 in Little Thurlow, Suffolk and his father dying only a few weeks after he was born he laid the foundations for what thrives to this day as the newspapers, books and retail chain WH Smith.

Shortly before his birth, his parents had established a news vending business in Little Grosvenor Street, London, and Smith later went into partnership in the business with his mother and brother. Following his mother's death, the business was divided between the brothers and, with William Henry Smith proving the most business-minded, the firm accordingly became known as W. H. Smith.

The business rapidly expanded under his guidance, with outlets, for example, in railway stations and, in 1846, it became WH Smith & Son – trading today as WH Smith plc – after he admitted his son as a partner; he died in 1865.

In the sciences, Robert Angus Smith was the Scottish chemist and early environmentalist credited as having, through his research into air pollution, been the first to describe what is now known as acid rain.

Born in 1817 in Pollokshaws, Glasgow, he studied chemistry at both Glasgow University and in Germany, later joining the chemical laboratory at the Royal Manchester Institution.

It was at Manchester, recognised as the world's first industrial city, that Smith, at first working with the institute and then as an independent analytical chemist, discovered the corrosive effect on the environment of acid rain caused by industrial pollution.

His pioneering work *Air and Rain: the Beginnings of a Chemical Climatology* was published in 1872; known today as the "Father of Acid Rain", he died in 1884.

Knighted in 1909 for his services to children, Sir William Smith was the Scot who founded the Boys' Brigade. Born in 1854 in Thurso, on the north coast of the Highlands, the family moved to Glasgow following his father's death in 1868, and where he later entered his uncle's wholesale dealership in soft goods.

Commissioned into the Rifle Volunteers and later the Lanarkshire Rifle Volunteers, he was also a Sunday school teacher with the Church of Scotland.

Combining aspects of the military with his deeply held Christian beliefs, it was in Glasgow in October of 1883 that he formed the Boys' Brigade.

He died in 1914, while there is a memorial stone to him in St Paul's Cathedral, London and in St Giles' Cathedral, Edinburgh.

In twentieth century British politics, John Smith was the Labour Party politician who served as its leader from July of 1992 until his death in May of 1994

Born in 1938 in Dalmally, Argyll and Bute, the son of a headmaster, and growing up in Ardrishaig, he studied history at Glasgow University from 1956 to 1959 and then, from 1959 to 1962, law.

An enthusiastic and skilled debater at university, he won, along with his debating partner Gordon Hunter, the coveted Observer Mace debating competition in 1962 – and his debating skills truly came to the fore when he entered Parliament.

This was in 1970 when, after having been admitted to Scotland's Faculty of Advocates and practising for a time as a solicitor, he was elected Member of Parliament (MP) for North Lanarkshire.

Top government posts he held before being elected Labour Party leader included Under Secretary of State at the Department of Energy, while as Leader of the House of Commons he was responsible for steering through the proposals for devolution for Scotland and Wales.

Elected Labour leader following the resignation of Neil Kinnock after the party was defeated in the 1992 General Election, one of his important initiatives was, at the 1993 party conference, managing to abolish the trade union block vote at conferences.

It was shortly after delivering a speech at the

Park Lane Hotel, London in May of 1994 – in which he stated: "The opportunity to serve our country, that is all we ask" – that he died after suffering a heart attack.

Interred on the island of Iona, sacred burial place of a number of Scottish kings, he is survived by his wife Elizabeth, who was created Baroness Smith of Gilmorehill, and daughters Sarah, a television news journalist, Catherine, a lawyer and Jane, a costume designer.

Attracting a decidedly different type of fame, Anna Nicole Smith was the former American model, actress and television personality born Vickie Lynn Hogan in Houston, Texas, in 1967.

Playmate magazine's Playmate of the Year in 1993, a year later the 26-year-old Smith married the 89-year-old oil tycoon Howard Marshall.

The marriage lasted only 14 months, until his death at the age of 90, and a bitter legal battle ensued between family from his first marriage and his young widow over the terms of his will.

Anna, after being awarded $474m by the courts, later reduced to $88m, died in 2007 as a result of an overdose from prescription drugs, while the legal wrangling over Marshall's wealth continues to this day.

Chapter four:

On the world stage

Fondly nicknamed "The Girl with the Curls", "America's Sweetheart" and "Little Mary", Gladys Louise Smith was the major star of the early silver screen era better known by her stage name of Mary Pickford.

Born in Toronto in 1892, the future Canadian-American actress's mother, Charlotte, worked as a seamstress while separated from her husband and took in boarders.

By chance, one of these boarders was a theatre manager who, struck by young Gladys's looks, gave her some small stage roles.

Her mother and two younger siblings also had acting talent, and the manager arranged for them to tour the theatre circuit throughout the United States, travelling from town to town and city to city by rail.

By the time she was aged 15, the talented and precocious Gladys had landed a supporting role in a Broadway production, *The Warrens of Virginia*, with the producer insisting that she adopt the stage name of Mary Pickford.

It was as Mary Pickford that she subsequently went on to star in 52 films throughout her career.

Early silent era films include the 1909 *Sweet and Twenty* and *To Save Her Soul*, and they quickly made her a star.

Often playing a child in her films, such as in the 1917 *The Poor Little Rich Girl*, the 1917 *Rebecca of Sunnybrook Farm* and, from 1918, *Little Lord Fauntleroy*, she played a more adult role in the 1929 *Coquette* – winning an Academy Award for Best Actress.

Her many fans were dismayed, however, that for her role in *Coquette* she had her famous curly blond locks cut into a bob – an act that made front page news.

Married for a time to the actor Douglas Fairbanks, with whom she toured throughout the United States, along with other celebrities during the First World War to promote the sale of Liberty Bonds to aid America's war effort, it was along with Fairbanks, Charlie Chaplin and the film director D.W. Griffith that she founded the film company United Artists.

Later married, in 1937, to the band leader Buddy Rogers, she went into retirement having previously also founded the Motion Picture Relief Fund for impoverished actors.

She sadly became an alcoholic, but survived to the age of 87 – the recipient of a host of awards and honours that include, three years before her death in 1979, an Academy Award for Lifetime Achievement.

Also the posthumous recipient of a star on Canada's Walk of Fame in her native Toronto, the Mary Pickford Theater at the Library of Congress, Washington, D.C., is named in her honour.

Her brother Jack and sister Lottie also adopted the Pickford stage name and followed successful careers in film, although their careers were largely overshadowed by that of their more famous sister.

In contemporary times, Willard Carroll Smith, Jr., is the American actor, producer and rapper better known as **Will Smith**.

Born in 1968, it was as The Fresh Prince, that he performed as a rapper, later going on to star from 1990 to 1996 in his own television show, *The Fresh Prince of Bel-Air*.

The recipient of Academy Award nominations for the 2001 film *Ali* and the 2006 *The Pursuit of Happyness*, other major screen credits include the

1996 *Independence Day*, the 1997 *Men in Black* and, from 2012, Men in Black III.

Other credits include the 2007 *I Am Legend* and, from 2013, *After Earth*.

Born in 1934 in Ilford, Essex, Margaret Natalie Smith is the multi-award-winning English actress better known as **Maggie Smith**, and more formally, as **Dame Maggie Smith**.

Beginning her stage career in 1952, her theatre awards include three Tony Award nominations – for the 1975 production of *Private Lives*, the 1979 *Night and Day* and, from 1990, *Lettice and Lovage*.

On the screen, the veteran actress is the recipient of a number of awards that include an Academy Award for Best Actress for the 1969 *The Prime of Miss Jean Brodie* and a nomination for Best Supporting Actress for the 1975 *California Suite*.

Also starring as Professor Minerva McGonagall in the *Harry Potter* series of films, her many television roles include that of Violet Crawley, Dowager Countess of Grantham, in *Downton Abbey*.

Born in 1969 in The Bronx, New York, **Allison Smith** is the American actress best known for her role of Mallory O'Brien in the television series *The West Wing*.

Other television credits include the 1980s' sitcom *Kate and Allie*, *Nip/Tuck* and *CSI: Crime Scene Investigation*, while she also played the title role in a Broadway production of *Annie*.

Born in Allen, Texas, in 1981, **Brian J. Smith** is the American actor who, best known for his role of Lieutenant Matthew Scott in the *Stargate* television series, also won a Drama Desk Award nomination for Outstanding Featured Actor in a Play for his role in a Broadway production of Tennessee Williams' *The Glass Menagerie*.

Best known for her role of Dr Erica Hahn in the American television medical series *Grey's Anatomy*, **Brooke Smith**, born in New York in 1967, also appeared in the 1991 film *Silence of the Lambs*.

On British television screens, **Benjamin Smith**, born in 1989 in Edgeware, London, is the actor known for his role from 2001 to 2003 of Del Trotter's son, Damien, in the popular sitcom *Only Fools and Horses*.

Other television credits include *Goodnight Mister Tom*, starring beside the late John Thaw, *Sherlock Holmes and the Baker Street Irregulars*, *Holby City* and *Misfits*.

Born in 1954 in Bermondsey, London, Brian

Arthur John Smith is the English alternative comedian and writer better known as **Arthur Smith**.

A regular on the stand-up comedy circuit, including the annual Edinburgh Festival Fringe, in addition to writing stage plays such as *An Evening with Gary Lineker*, he has also appeared on the television series *Grumpy Old Men* and hosted *Arthur Smith's Comedy Club* on BBC Radio 4 Extra.

Back on American shores, **Charles Martin Smith**, born in 1953 in Van Nuys, California, is the actor, writer and director whose big screen credits include the 1973 *American Graffiti*, the 1984 *Starman* and the 1987 *The Untouchables*, while he also wrote and directed the 2011 *Dolphin Tale*.

Bearers of the Smith name have also excelled in the highly competitive world of sport.

Born in Portsmouth in 1984, **Andrew Smith** is the English badminton player who, in both 2004 and 2005, won the New Zealand International, while on the fields of European football, Cameron Smith, born in 1995 and better known as **Cammy Smith**, is the Scottish player who, after having come through its youth system, made his debut for Scottish Premiership club Aberdeen in 2012.

Possessed with truly impressive physical

strength, **Adrian Smith**, born in 1964, is the former strongman and competitor for Great Britain who won the title of UK's Strongest Man in 1990, 1992, 1997 and 1998.

Taking to the water, one particularly intrepid bearer of the Smith name is **Joe Smith**, who holds the record as the oldest man to have swum the English Channel.

Born in Rochdale, Lancashire, he was aged 65 when he achieved the feat in September of 1999 in a time of 14 hours and nine minutes.

Now resident in Deal, Kent, he was honoured by being selected as a torch bearer through Deal for the 2012 London Olympics.

From sport to music, **Reginald Leonard Smith**, born in 1939 in Blackheath, London is the English singer, songwriter and record producer better known as **Marty Wilde**.

One of the leading British rock and roll singers of the late 1950s with his band the Wildcats, he was later responsible for writing or co-writing a string of hits for other artists that include Bobby Vee's *Rubber Ball*, Don Gibson's *Sea of Heartbreak*, Lulu's *I'm a Tiger* and Status Quo's *Ice in the Sun*.

Married to Joyce Baker, formerly of the singing and dancing group the Vernon Girls, he is the father of the pop singers **Ricky**, **Roxanne** and **Kim Wilde**.

Born in 1960, Kim Wilde has enjoyed international chart success with hits that include her 1981 single *Kids in America*, while in 1983 she won a BRIT Award for Best British Female Solo Artist.

Known as "Mister Country", **Carl Smith** was the American country music singer born in 1927 in Maynardville, Tennessee.

Married for a time to June Carter – who later married fellow country singer Johnny Cash – he enjoyed success with hit singles that include his 1951 *Let's Live a Little*, *If Teardrops Were Pennies* and *Let Old Mother Nature Have Her Way*; a member of the Country Music Hall of Fame, he died in 2010.

Born in 1938 in Houston, Texas, **James Marcus Smith** is the American singer, songwriter and actor better known as **P.J. Proby**.

With hit singles that include *Somewhere*, *Hold Me* and *Maria*, his stage credits include his portrayal of Elvis Presley in *Elvis – The Musical*, winner of a Best Musical of the Year Award in 1985.

Born in 1906 in Calumet, Michigan, **Paul J.**

Smith was the American film music composer who won an Academy Award for Best Original Score for the 1940 *Pinocchio*; he died in 1985 and was later honoured as a Disney Legend.

From music to the equally creative world of the written word, R. Alexander "Sandy" McCall Smith, better known to his readers as **Alexander McCall Smith**, is the prolific British author and expert on medical law.

Born in 1948 in Bulawayo, in what was then Rhodesia, now Zimbabwe, his many academic posts have included Emeritus Professor of Law at Edinburgh University.

Now resident in Edinburgh, he is best known for his best-selling series of novels and short stories that include the *No.1 Ladies' Detective Agency*, *44 Scotland Street*, *The Sunday Philosophy Club*, *Corduroy Mansions* and *Professor Dr von Igelfeld Entertainments*.

Awarded the prestigious Cholmondeley Award for Poets in 1996 and best known for her poem *Not Waving But Drowning*, Florence Margaret Smith was the English poet and novelist better known as **Stevie Smith**.

Born in 1902 in Kingston upon Hull and the

recipient in 1969 of the Queen's Gold Medal for Poetry, she died in 1971.

In the decidedly mysterious world of the paranormal, **Christopher Neil-Smith** was the Anglican priest who exorcised an estimated 3,000 supposed demons from tormented souls throughout England until some years before his death in 1995.

Born in 1920 in Hampstead, London and a vicar at St Saviour's Anglican Church in North London, he came to particular media attention – often being interviewed on the subject – following the release in 1973 of the film *The Exorcist*, based on the novel of the name by William Peter Blatty.

Officially authorised by the Bishop of London in 1972 to exorcise demons 'according to his own judgement' – although he had been carrying out exorcisms since at least 1949 – he died in 1995.